MASSACHUSETTS LANDLORD-TENANT PRACTICE: LAW AND FORMS –

SECURITY DEPOSITS
AND
LAST MONTH'S RENT

G. EMIL WARD, ESQ.

ISBN: 978-0-615-49124-0

52490

9 780615 491240

Contact us at: eward@wardlawonline.com
www.wardlawonline.com
(617) 202-5200

TABLE OF CONTENTS

i

§ 1. Security Deposits, Last Month's Rent; Access to Apartment; Records; Receipts.

MASS. GEN. LAWS ch. 186, § 15B is disjointed, perhaps seeking to accomplish too much and has probably resulted in the elimination, as a practical matter, of security deposits. This is so because a landlord who attempts to comply with the rigid requirements of the statute will, in this author's opinion, expend more time and effort and will likely incur more exposure to multiple damages and attorney's fees for improper handling than the single month's rent could possibly mitigate in damage to the apartment, for lost rent or unpaid water bills. The statute has been held to be internally ambiguous especially as to remedies available for violations of different parts of the statute. The reasons will become clear as the statute's explanation unfolds below.

§ 1(a). Remedies Generally.

Section 15B contains some provisions which are self-enforcing, which merely require immediate return of the tenant's money if a landlord fails to comply with the statute[1] and others which impose multiple damages and attorney's fees.[2] Regardless, where the landlord is deemed to be engaged in trade or commerce, the Attorney General's Landlord-Tenant Regulations authorize tenants to seek to establish liability and collect damages under Chapter 93A.[3]

---

[1] MASS. GEN. LAWS ch. 186, § 15B(3)(a).
[2] MASS. GEN. LAWS ch. 186, § 15B(7).
[3] Mass. Regs. Code tit. 940 § 3.01, § 3.16(1)-(4) and § 3.17(3)(b) and (4); *see also* § 3.17(1), (2), (5) and (6).

§ 2. Amounts Landlord May Collect at Inception of Tenancy.

At the beginning of a tenancy, the landlord may collect a maximum of three months' rent and the cost of purchase and installation of a lock and key, as follows: the first month's rent, the last month's rent, and a security deposit not greater than the first month's rent.[4] However, as explained below, landlords must scrupulously follow escrow requirements in order to lawfully collect and retain a security deposit.[5]

§ 3. Security Deposit; Property of Tenant.

Chapter 186, § 15B is dedicated to the proposition that the security deposit, although given to the landlord, is given so in trust and remains at all times the property of the tenant, until lawfully and properly drawn down by the landlord.[6] It must be escrowed[7] so as to protect it from claims of the landlord, to prevent it from being commingled with the landlord's assets, and to protect it from claims of creditors of the landlord, such as foreclosing mortgagees or bankruptcy trustees.[8]

---

[4] MASS. GEN. LAWS ch. 186, §15B(1)(b).

[5] MASS. GEN. LAWS ch. 186, § 15B(2), (3).

[6] MASS. GEN. LAWS ch. 186, § 15B (1) (e): "A security deposit shall continue to be the property of the tenant making such deposit, shall not be commingled with the assets of the lessor, and shall not be subject to the claims of any creditor of the lessor or of the lessor's successor in interest, including a foreclosing mortgagee or trustee in bankruptcy;...."

[7] MASS. GEN. LAWS ch. 186, §15B(3).

[8] MASS. GEN. LAWS ch. 186, § 15B(1)(e) and (3)(a).

§ 3(a). Requirement of Receipt.

Within thirty days of receiving the deposit, the landlord must give the tenant a receipt indicating the amount of the deposit, the name and location of the bank, and the account number.[9]

PRACTICE POINTER

The requirements regarding taking, keeping, and accounting for security deposits are so onerous as to discourage all but the most stout of heart from requiring a security deposit of a tenant at all. Further, in this weak economy, even though a landlord has a right to collect up to 3 months' rent and the cost of a key and lock installation at the inception of a tenancy, such a landlord probably puts the apartment at a competitive disadvantage. For it is axiomatic that a tenant would sooner pay two months' rent to secure an apartment than three. For these reasons, a landlord should think twice before asking for a security deposit in addition to a first and last month's rent. The author often advises that due to the above, a security deposit should be waived with two possible exceptions: (1) tenants with pets; and (2) undergraduate students.

In all other instances a landlord must rely upon credit reports, references from landlords at least one landlord prior to the tenant's present one, criminal record checks, a verified good source of income for the tenant, signed in-state guarantees, attorney's fees provisions and similar protections.

---

[9] MASS. GEN. LAWS ch. 186, §§ 15B(2)(b) and (3)(a).

§ 3(b). Security Deposit Escrow Requirements; In-State Bank.

The security deposit must be placed in a "separate, interest-bearing account" in a Massachusetts bank protected from the claims of the landlord's creditors including a foreclosing lender or bankruptcy trustee and under terms "as will provide for its transfer to a subsequent owner of said property."[10] Although the bank may be an interstate bank, the branch where the security deposit account is opened must be a branch physically located within Massachusetts' borders.[11] Section 15B(3)(a) requires the landlord to arrange with the bank for automatic transfer to a successor owner, such that upon presentation of proper proof of change in ownership of the premises, the bank may readily, i.e., without litigation, transfer the account to the next owner. Presently this may be done by simply designating the account a tenant's security deposit or tenant's trust account. By operation of MASS. GEN. LAWS ch. 167D, § 32 such accounts comply with the requirements of MASS. GEN. LAWS ch. 186 § 15B(3)(a).

The Appeals Court has held that a landlord will not violate MASS. GEN. LAWS ch. 186, § 15B (1)(e) or § 15B (3)(a) where his or her agent commingles the security deposit and last month's rent, so long as he or she maintains these two types of monies in a bank account separate from the one in which the landlord's own funds are placed, which cannot be attached by his creditors, uses an accounting system to track the security deposit, last month's rent and interest due, and the landlord is unable to access the last month's rent until

---

[10] MASS. GEN. LAWS ch.186, § 15B(3)(a).
[11] Taylor v. Burke, 69 Mass.App.Ct. 77, 79-80, 866 N.E.2d 911, 914-15 (2007); MASS. GEN. LAWS ch.186, § 15B(3)(a).

it is due and owing.[12] This arrangement ensures the primary purposes of the statute will be carried out—namely, protection of the tenant's funds from conversion to the landlord's personal use, proper crediting of interest to the tenant where applicable, and placement of the funds beyond the reach of the landlord's creditors.

Under the above-described system, these objectives were met and therefore there was no violation of the statute. The Appeals Court went on to find that although, to a degree, the last month's rent, with certain limitations, is the property of the landlord under the above-referenced circumstances, where the last month's rent was not readily available to the landlord but rather was only used as a last month's rent, the arrangement described above was not a violation of the statute.

§ 3(c). Remedy.

"Failure to comply with this paragraph [(3)(a), requiring a receipt for escrowed security deposit] shall entitle the tenant to immediate return of the security deposit."[13]

"Failure to [properly deposit the tenant's money] shall entitle the tenant to immediate return of the security

---

[12] Neihaus v. Maxwell, 54 Mass.App.Ct. 558, 561-62, 776 N.E.2d 556, 558-59 (2002).

[13] MASS. GEN. LAWS ch. 186, § 15B (3)(a). Mass. Regs. Code tit. 940, § 3.16 (3), a general provision imposing 93A liability for failures to comply with laws protecting residential tenants, and 3.17 (4)(b) require the same type of receipts the statute requires and impose 93A liability: "[Whoever] fail[s] to give to the tenant a written receipt indicating...the amount of the security deposit, if any, paid by the tenant, in accordance with M.G.L. c. 186, § 15B" is liable under Chapter 93A.

deposit."[14] Further, a tenant is entitled to treble damages if, upon demand and failure to receive the deposit, the tenant is forced to file suit and to further pursue the litigation against the landlord, because the deposit was still not immediately returned.[15]

§ 4. Interest Due on Security Deposits.

Interest at the rate of 5% or whatever lesser amount the landlord actually earns per annum on the security deposit must be paid to the tenant at the end of each year. Alternatively, the landlord may notify the tenant at the end of each year that the tenant may deduct the interest due from the next month's rent. If the landlord fails, after thirty days from the anniversary of each tenancy to pay or give notice as described above, the tenant may simply deduct the amount due.

If the tenancy terminates before the anniversary date, interest runs from the start of the tenancy and is paid pro-rata for time the deposit was retained.[16] Further, on the

---

[14] MASS. GEN. LAWS ch. § 186, 15B(3)(a). Chapter 93A remedies are imposed by Mass. Regs. Code tit. 940, § 3.17(4)(d) and § 3.16(1), (3)-(4).
[15] Castenholz v. Caira, 21 Mass.App.Ct. 758, 762-64, 490 N.E.2d 494, 497-98 (1986). A landlord who failed to properly escrow the security deposit within thirty days after receipt of same and further failed to promptly return the deposit to the tenant upon the tenant's demand, was liable for the amount of treble damages, costs and attorney's fees. The decision was based upon the landlord's failure to promptly return the deposit after commencement of the action, thereby forcing the tenant to litigate further. Additionally, the court held that commencement of suit acted as the tenant's demand. MASS. GEN. LAWS. ch. 186, § 15B(3)(a), 6(a), (7).
[16] MASS. GEN. LAWS ch. 186, § 15B(3)(b): "[I]n the event that the tenancy is terminated before the anniversary date of the

anniversary of the tenancy, a statement must be sent to the tenant containing the name and address of the bank, the amount of deposit, the account number, and the interest due on the security deposit.[17] Failure to properly deposit in a bank branch physically located in Massachusetts pursuant to § 15B(3)(a) exposes the landlord to treble damages.[18] This is in addition to forfeiture of the right to retain any portion of the security deposit or to counterclaim in the tenant's action for return of the deposit.[19]

PRACTICE POINTER

There is no requirement that the landlord must open a separate escrow account for each security deposit taken for each separate dwelling. Rather it appears sufficient if one account is kept and the proper record keeping is undertaken. However, it is good practice to segregate escrow deposits per property deed and not to commingle the deposits of many properties within one security deposit account. This is so not because of case or statutory requirement, but because as a practical matter the more the landlord does to facilitate compliance with the statute and to make the accounting as transparent as possible, the more likely the landlord is to avoid the treble damage provisions of § 15B(3)(a), (6)(a) and (7).

No statute or case requires that the landlord pay a tenant more than the 5% annually on the security deposit.

---

tenancy, the tenant shall receive all accrued interest within thirty days of such termination."

[17] MASS. GEN. LAWS ch. 186, § 15B(3)(b).

[18] Taylor v. Burke, 69 Mass.App.Ct. 77, 86, 866 N.E.2d 911, 918 (2007); MASS. GEN. LAWS ch. 186, § 15B(3)(a), 6(a), (7).

[19] Jinwala v. Bizzaro, 24 Mass.App.Ct. 1, 6, 505 N.E.2d 904, 907 (1987); MASS. GEN. LAWS. ch. 186, § 15B(3)(a), (6)-(7).

Therefore, the landlord may retain for his own account to be removed annually (in order to avoid commingling) any amount in excess of the statutory interest rate. In these times of low interest rates, however, there will be no excess. However, if interest rates exceed 5% on such accounts, the "dividend" to the landlord is some, though paltry, recompense for the comparatively large administrative burdens imposed on security deposits.

§ 4(a). Statement of Conditions.

The next requirement of a landlord's taking and retaining a security deposit mandates that the landlord "shall, upon receipt of such security deposit, or within ten days after commencement of the tenancy, whichever is later," give the tenant or prospective tenant a written statement of conditions. The statement must contain a comprehensive list of all then-existing damage to the unit and must be signed by the lessor or his or her agent.

The statement must provide a statutory caveat in 12-point boldface type directing the tenant to sign the statement of conditions if it is correct, or to resubmit his or her own list if the landlord's statement is not accurate. This must be done by the tenant within fifteen days of receipt of the statement of conditions or of move-in. The statement must inform the tenant or prospective tenant that failure to resubmit any list may allow a court to view such tenant's failure as his or her agreement as to the completeness of the landlord's proposed statement of conditions.

The landlord then has fifteen days from receipt of the tenant's proposed list of damages to sign off in agreement or to send a clear statement of disagreement.[20]

§ 4(b). Remedy.

No direct monetary penalty is imposed by § 15B for failure to issue the statement of conditions. However, the Attorney General's regulations, as previously stated are violated by the landlord's failure to submit a statement of conditions. Thus, 93A damages, attorney's fees and costs may be awarded even if the damages are only the nominal statutory amount of $25.00.[21] Further, the landlord is required to immediately return the deposit for failure to give the statement of conditions upon the tenant's demand. In turn, failure to pay the security deposit or the balance then due within a reasonable time of demand is a violation of the triple damages provisions. [22]

§ 5. Records of Security Deposit; Availability to Tenants and Prospective Tenants.

All landlords must maintain records of the security deposits containing information described below for two years after termination of the tenancy or occupancy and must make them available to the tenant "or prospective tenant" for inspection during the landlord's normal business hours. The

---

[20] MASS. GEN. LAWS ch. 186, § 15B(2)(c).

[21] Mass. Regs. Code tit. 940, § 3.17(4)(e).

[22] MASS. GEN. LAWS ch. 186, § 15B(1)(b)(iii): A landlord may take a security deposit "provided that...the tenant is given a statement of conditions as required by subsection (2)"; *Id.*; see Section 3(c) above.

statute requires the landlord to retain the four following categories of information:

> (i)   a "detailed description of any damage done to ...the dwelling units";

> (ii)   "the date upon which the occupancy of the tenant...charged with such damage was terminated";

> (iii)   "the dates of repairs, [if any], the cost thereof, and receipts therefor";

> (iv)   copies of receipts or statements of conditions given to tenants or prospective tenants.

§ 5(a). Remedy.

"Upon a wrongful failure by the lessor...to make such record available...for a tenant or prospective tenant, [either of them] shall be entitled to the immediate return of any...security deposit together with any interest which has accrued thereon."[23]

---

[23] MASS. GEN. LAWS ch. 186, § 15B(2)(d)(iii). Additionally, such a failure would violate Chapter 93A through the mechanism of the Attorney General's regulations. It is a Chapter 93A violation for a landlord to "(k) otherwise fail to comply with the provisions of M.G.L. c. 186, § 15B." Mass. Regs. Code tit. 940, § 3.17(4)(k). *See also Id.*, § 3.16(3). It is a violation of Chapter 93A if "[the wrongful act] fails to comply with existing statutes, rules, regulations or laws, meant for the protection of the public's health, safety, or welfare promulgated by the Commonwealth."

§ 6. Landlord's Forfeiture of Retention of Security Deposit; Loss of Counterclaim.

If the landlord has violated the statue, he or she loses the right to counterclaim in the tenant's action for return of the security deposit. In any violation of the security deposit statute wherein the landlord is required to immediately forfeit retention of the security deposit and to forfeit the right to assert counterclaims which could ordinarily be alleged in a suit brought by the tenant for the return of the security deposit, the statutory scheme "does not prevent a landlord from prosecuting an independent action to recover damages for abuse of the rental premises." Further, the landlord is not barred by the rules of issue preclusion in this event. The purpose of this scheme is to guarantee the tenant an untrammeled and inexpensive return of his or her security deposit when the landlord has violated certain parts of the statute, not to deprive the landlord of a remedy for property damage.[24]

§ 7. Four Allowable Deductions; Return of Security Deposit Within Thirty Days.

Within thirty days of termination of "occupancy" of a tenancy at will or at "the end of the tenancy as specified in a valid written lease agreement," the landlord must return "the security deposit or any balance thereof" and may deduct for the four items listed below. "No deduction may be made from the security deposit for any purpose other than those set

---

[24] Jinwala v. Bizzaro, 24 Mass.App.Ct. 1, 6-7, 505 N.E.2d 904, 907 (1987) (although right to counterclaim for damage to premises in tenant's suit for security deposit lost due to landlord's violation of MASS. GEN. LAWS ch. 186, § 15B(6)(a)-(e), landlord is not barred from bringing independent suit for damages).

forth in this section."[25] In that the purpose of the security deposit is to indemnify the landlord in some small degree against damage from certain allowable losses, it only makes sense that the thirty day period begins to run not from the technical end of a lease or tenancy but upon the end of the tenant's lawful occupancy. Otherwise the purpose of deducting for damages could not be fulfilled because one would not know the extent of damage until the tenant had finally and irrevocably surrendered actual possession. The Appeals Court has ruled definitively on the issue of when the thirty-day return period begins to run. "Again, we agree with the trial judge that Neihaus's obligation to return [the tenant's] security deposit within thirty days did not arise at the expiration of the written lease but, rather, when they relinquished possession."[26]

The only four lawful deductions are for:

"(i) any unpaid rent or water charges [which have been properly implemented through the sub-metering provisions] which have not been validly withheld or deducted pursuant to [law]"; and[27]

---

[25] MASS. GEN. LAWS ch. 186, § 15B(4).

[26] Neihaus v. Maxwell, 54 Mass.App.Ct. 558, 562, 776 N.E.2d 556, 559 (2002).

[27] MASS. GEN. LAWS ch. 186 § 15B(4)(i). *See* Share Loan Fund of Alcoholism & Drug Abuse Found, Inc. v. Upright, 1996 Mass. App. Div. 163 (1996) (Landlord did not violate provisions of security deposit statute when landlord deducted unpaid rent from tenant's security deposit and therefore tenant's assignee had no claim against landlord under the statute).

12

"(ii) any unpaid increase in real estate taxes [imposed pursuant to a valid tax escalation clause pursuant to Chapter 186 § 15C]"; and[28]

"(iii) a reasonable amount necessary to repair any damage caused to the dwelling unit by the tenant or any person under the tenant's control or on the premises with the tenant's consent," reasonable wear and tear excluded."[29]

The landlord must also provide to the tenant within thirty days of surrender of possession, the following:

(i) "an itemized list of damages, sworn to by the lessor or his agent under the pains and penalties of perjury"[30];

(ii) "[a detailed itemization of] the nature of the damage and of the repairs necessary to correct such damage"; and

---

[28] MASS. GEN. LAWS ch. 186, § 15B(4)(ii). Chapter 186, § 15C, requires, that no residential lease may require increased tax payments from the tenant unless three conditions are met: (i) that the tenant pay only the proportion of the increase that his or her unit bears to the entire real estate tax assessed, (ii) that the exact percentage of the increase imposed upon the tenant be stated in the lease, and (iii) that the lessor will return a pro-rata share of any abatement obtained by the lessor, less reasonable attorney's fees. This provision may not be waived by landlord and tenant, as waiver is deemed to be against public policy. Lastly, if the landlord mistakenly collects an increase in excess of the tenant's actual pro-rata share that excess shall be returned with 5% interest due per annum from the date of collection.
[29] MASS. GEN. LAWS ch. 186, § 15B(4)(iii).
[30] Id.

(iii) "written evidence, such as estimates, bills, invoices or receipts, indicating the actual or estimated cost [of the repairs]."[31]

The landlord may not deduct for damage listed on the statement of conditions or the tenant-submitted statement of conditions "unless the lessor subsequently repaired or caused to be repaired said damage and can prove that the renewed damage was unrelated to the prior damage and was caused by the tenant or by any person under the tenant's control or on the premises with the tenant's consent."[32]

By clear statutory language the landlord is not limited to recovering only the amount of the security deposit if the amount of damage "willfully or maliciously" worked upon the real or personal property of the landlord exceeds the amount of the security deposit.[33]

Taylor v. Beaudry[34] recently made clear that "the landlord was entitled to deduct damage repair costs from the security deposit <u>only</u> if he complied with G.L. c. 186, § 15B(4)(iii)...which requires the landlord to provide the tenant", within thirty days of vacating the premises, an itemized, sworn list of damages, plus written proofs of estimates or of actual repairs. (emphasis added).

§ 7(a). Important Change in Landlord's Defenses; Castenholz Return of Security Deposit No Longer a Remedy for All Violations of § 15B(6).

---

[31] *Id.*
[32] *Id.*
[33] MASS. GEN. LAWS ch. 186, § 15B(4)(iii).
[34] 75 Mass.App.Ct. 411, 416, 914 N.E.2d 931, 935-36 (2009).

Very recently the Appeals Court rendered a decision in *Taylor v. Beaudry* (see note 34), which will upset the standard practice of returning the tenant's security deposit when the landlord has violated any of the treble damage provisions of the statute, even if the return occurred beyond the thirty day period. Until *Taylor*, this was the fairly standard procedure recommended to those landlords lucky enough to have counsel knowledgeable in security deposit remedies.

In *Castenholz v. Caira,*[35] the court held that where the landlord failed to place the security deposit in an interest bearing escrow account within thirty days of receiving it, and then failed to return the deposit to the tenant within a reasonable time after demand, the landlord was liable for treble damages, interest, costs, and a reasonable attorney's fee. See footnote 15 above; Section 8 below.

"We think, then, that the *Castenholz* framework is inapplicable to the landlord's failure to return the tenant's security deposit within the specified thirty days. The statutory obligation to return the deposit is clear, as is the time within which the deposit must be returned. Equally unambiguous are the consequences of failing to comply with that [30 day] deadline." *Taylor v. Beaudry.*[36]

Where the landlord has failed "to return to the tenant the security deposit or balance thereof to which the tenant is entitled after deducting therefrom any sums in accordance with the provisions of [§15B(6)(e)], together with any interest thereon, within thirty days after termination of the

---

[35] 21 Mass.App.Ct. 758, 763-64, 490 N.E.2d 494, 497-98 (1986).
[36] 75 Mass.App.Ct. 411, 416, 914 N.E.2d 931, 935-36 (2009).

tenancy,"[37] this failure shall subject the landlord to "damages in an amount equal to three times the amount of such security deposit or balance thereof to which the tenant is entitled," plus interest from the date the payment was due, reasonable attorney's fees and costs.[38] (internal quotations omitted).

§ 7(b). Remedy.

Upon the landlord's failure to properly and timely return the security deposit or balance thereof such a wronged tenant "shall be awarded damages in an amount equal to three times the amount of such security deposit or balance thereof to which the tenant is entitled," along with 5% interest from the due date, court costs, and reasonable attorney's fees.[39]

PRACTICE POINTER

Although there is no case directly on point, considering the policy behind the stringent triple damage provisions for failure to properly account for and/or return the security deposit within thirty days, it would appear that the landlord must make and be prepared to prove all good faith efforts to, in fact, deliver the balance of the security deposit to the tenant within thirty days from the time the tenant actually vacates the premises.[40]

---

[37] MASS. GEN. LAWS. ch. 186, § 15B(6)(e).

[38] Taylor v. Beaudry, 75 Mass.App.Ct. 411, 417, 914 N.E.2d 931, 936 (2009).

[39] MASS. GEN. LAWS ch. 186, § 15B(6)(e),(7).

[40] *Cf.* Mellor v. Berman, 390 Mass. 275, 279, 454 N.E.2d 907, 911 (1983) (Treble damages award for improper retention of part of security deposit not conditioned on finding of bad faith or wilful violation of the statute); Hampshire Village Associates v. District Court of Hampshire, 381 Mass. 148, 408 N.E.2d 830 (1980), *cert.*

It is advisable, therefore, that if the tenant vacates without leaving a forwarding address, the landlord must attempt to send the tenant's money order and required records by certified mail, return receipt requested, to the old address in the hope that it will be forwarded by the post office. Or, by writing to the postmaster of the recently vacated apartment, one might obtain the forwarding address of the tenant, if one was left, and then forward the security deposit and required documents directly to the tenant by way of certified mail, return receipt requested. In this way, assuming the landlord has complied with all other accounting and return requirements, the landlord has done all that was reasonably possible to "return" the tenant's security deposit.

§ 7(c). Deductions; Lack of Good Faith.

The deduction and return provisions impose strict liability for failure to comply and do not condition liability for improper retention of a part of the security deposit on "a finding of bad faith or wilful violations by the lessor."[41]

---

denied, 449 U.S. 1062 (1980) (Award of treble damages for landlord's remittance to tenant of balance of security deposit on September 18 after tenant vacated the apartment in "early August" of the same year.)

[41] Mellor v. Berman, 390 Mass. 275, 279, 454 N.E.2d 907, 911 (1983). *See* In re Bologna, 206 B.R. 628, 633 (Bankr. D. Mass. 1997) (Under Massachusetts security deposit statute, award of damages for failing to comply with security deposit requirement requires no showing of fault or intent).

§ 8. Failure to Return Security Deposit Within Reasonable Time of Demand; Defense.

Where the landlord violates the provisions of MASS. GEN. LAWS ch. 186, § 15B(6) for failing to properly escrow the tenant's funds, a violation which requires forfeiture of the right to retain any portion of the security deposit and forfeiture of the right to counterclaim *in a tenant's action for return under subsection* (6), if the tenant then makes demand for its return while still residing in the property, the landlord may avoid the treble damages penalty and limit exposure to single damages if upon demand the security deposit is returned within a reasonable time after demand.[42]

---

[42] Castenholz v. Caira, 21 Mass. App. Ct. 758, 763-64, 490 N.E.2d 494, 497-98 (1986). Failure of the landlord to properly escrow security deposit within thirty days of receipt entitles tenant to immediate return upon demand. Where the landlords failed to properly escrow the security deposit, failed to pay proper interest, transferred the security deposit to their successors in interest, but failed to relieve themselves of liability for said deposit by failing to give the required notice of transfer, and where they then refused to pay out to the tenant the security deposit which they had previously transferred to their successor, they were nonetheless held liable for treble damages, interest, costs and attorney's fees. It was further held that the filing of suit itself operated as the tenant's demand. This author feels treble damages was an unduly harsh penalty in light of the fact that the tenants came to know of the transfer early in the "game" and no harm would have been done to them had they simply sued the new owner instead of the hapless former owner for a mere technical violation of the statute. Further, by transferring the security deposit to the new owner, the new owner received a windfall where there appears no order issued to force the new owner to disgorge the security deposit. Finally, the former owners seem to have paid treble damages AND lost the security deposit paid to the new owner. In short, such a tenant will suffer no actual damages so long as he or she is informed at some point of who holds the security deposit and can look to him or her

§ 8(a). Restrictive Endorsement; Not Proper Return.

Where the landlord improperly made deductions from the security deposit and attempted to place a restrictive endorsement or release on the back of the check for the balance of the deposit this was deemed "in substance a release of disputed claims written on [the check]...not, in our opinion...a tender of payment. [The tenant] has received a settlement offer, and that is not in accord with the text of G.L. c. 186, § 15B(4)."[43] After the landlord determines that her or she is entitled to make a deduction from the tenant's security deposit, he must strictly comply with the statutory requirements and "return the balance to the tenant without condition."[44] A tenant will be awarded three times the entire deposit, not simply the unreturned balance, plus costs and attorney's fees for the landlord's failure to comply with this provision.

§ 9. Transfer of Security Deposit.

A lessor must transfer the entire security deposit plus accrued interest to the successor in interest upon transfer of the "dwelling unit for which the deposit is held," if there is a "sale, assignment, death, appointment of receiver or trustee in bankruptcy, or otherwise." The successor in interest then becomes liable for "retention and return" from the date of transfer pursuant to § 15B. Upon transfer of the property to a

---

for the deposit. It was held that had the former owners returned the security deposit within a reasonable time following demand they would have avoided treble damages.

[43] Goes v. Feldman, 8 Mass.App.Ct. 84, 92, 391 N.E.2d 943, 948 (1979).

[44] *Id.*

new owner for any reason, even foreclosure, the new owner is bound by the amount of security deposit given and by rights accrued by the tenant under the prior owner, with limited exceptions. See section 9(f). [45]

§ 9(a). Exemption; Grant of Mortgage Not "Transfer" Under Statute.

The grant of a mortgage is expressly exempt from the definition of "transfer" under Chapter 186, § 15B(5), thus relieving a lender of any security deposit obligations resulting from the granting a mortgage.

§ 9(b). Notice from Successor in Interest.

Within forty-five days of the transfer, the successor in interest must notify the tenant that the security deposit was transferred to him or her and that he or she is holding it for the tenant's benefit. Notice must be written and must contain the successor's name, business address, business telephone number, and the name, business address, and business telephone number of the agent, if any. [46]

§ 9(c). Continuing Liability of Former Owner or Agent.

The former owner and his agent remain liable under § 15B (5), (7A) for retention, accounting for, and return of the security deposit, until one of the following occurs: (a) the security deposit has been transferred to the successor in

---

[45] MASS. GEN. LAWS ch. 186, § 15B(5).
[46] MASS. GEN. LAWS ch.186, § 15B(5)(a).

interest **AND** the tenant has been given the above-referenced written notice by the former owner or by the new owner; or (b) the deposit has been returned to the tenant.

§ 9(d). Liability of Successor in Interest for Transfer.

The successor in interest, except those described below, has full responsibility for compliance with the statute even if the former owner fails to transfer the security deposit to the successor "as required by this sub-section [(5)]."[47]

Where the buyers of a single family house completed purchase after the physical eviction of the tenants who had given a $1000 security deposit to the seller, where the seller failed to transfer the security deposit to the new owners, and where the new owners (buyers) failed, in turn, to pay the security deposit over to the evicted tenants within thirty days after their vacating, despite the fact that there was no tenancy in existence between the buyers and the evicted tenants and no transferred security deposit to return, under § 15B(6)(d) and (7) the buyers were held liable for treble damages.[48] Further, because the tenants had vacated the property, the successors in interest (buyers) could not discharge this

---

[47] MASS. GEN. LAWS ch. 186, § 15B(5). Although no appellate court has so held, it is likely that even a buyer at foreclosure sale is liable as a successor in interest just as if the property had been purchased at arm's length. The successor in interest "shall, without regard to the nature of the transfer, assume liability for payment of the security deposit" pursuant to § 15B.

[48] Vinton v. Demetrion, 19 Mass.App.Ct. 948, 949, 473 N.E.2d 207, 208 (1985). In passing, the court indicated that the buyers could have protected themselves against this liability by being aware of §15B(6)(d) and (7) and adjusting for the deposit, presumably at closing.

obligation by allowing the tenants to live "free" for one month.

The successor in interest may meet this obligation, however, if the tenant still resides on the premises, by granting "free use and occupancy" of the dwelling unit for the period of time equivalent to the amount of security deposit as "if the security deposit were deemed to be rent."[49]

§ 9(e). Failure to Transfer; Remedy; Defense.

While *Taylor v. Beaudry* [50] has thrown into disarray the classic *Castenholz* remedy for all violations of the security deposit statute, namely that of returning the deposit in the event of a claim of violation by the tenant, the Appeals Court did provide some indication that the treble damages provisions of subsection (7) would "likely" apply to a landlord's failure to properly transfer the security deposit pursuant to § 15B(6)(d). However, this was by no means a clear holding of the case. "[S]mooth application of § 15B(7) (the triple damages penalty provision of the statute) to § 15B(6)(d) (the forfeiture requirement of the statute where the landlord fails to properly transfer the security deposit to a successor in interest) *likely* requires the framework the court used in *Castenholz*." (emphasis added). (see note 50).

§ 9(f). Exemption from Transfer Liability: Municipalities and Banks.

A city or town which acquires a parcel of property through foreclosure of tax title or a "foreclosing mortgagee or

---

[49] MASS. GEN. LAWS ch. 186, § 15B(5).
[50] 75 Mass.App.Ct. 411, 416, N.E.2d, 931, 933 (2009).

a mortgagee in possession which is a financial institution chartered by the commonwealth or the United States" is expressly exempt from successor in interest liability if the former owner fails to transfer the security deposit in proper and timely fashion.[51]

§ 9(g). Small Claims Actions.

If the single damage amount of the security deposit is below the small claims jurisdictional maximum of $7,000, the tenant may use this expedited procedure to seek recovery either in the district court or the Housing Court small claims session. Venue is proper where either the plaintiff or defendant lives or has a usual place of business or employment, in addition to the plaintiff tenant's option to sue in the judicial district wherein the dwelling is located. It is the single damage amount that determines jurisdiction in small claims court. That court is, however, empowered to award treble damages, which exceed the jurisdictional threshold, without losing jurisdiction.[52]

PRACTICE POINTER

WARNING AGAINST LANDLORDS REMAINING IN SMALL CLAIMS COURT

In this author's opinion a landlord sued by a tenant in small claims court must opt out of the small claims procedure for several reasons. First, clerks are now empowered to hear these cases. Therefore, the trial is likely to take place before such an assistant clerk magistrate, not

---

[51] MASS. GEN LAWS ch. 186, § 15B(7A).
[52] *See* MASS. GEN. LAWS ch. 218, § 21.

before a judge. While most such clerks are familiar with the governing law, this author's recent experience with these hearings has been that the clerks tend to favor the tenant. Additionally, clerks tend to admit hearsay evidence of the type people DO NOT generally rely upon in making a decision, and the resulting harm is not easily rectified or excised from the finding. But, the more important reason is that if the landlord loses at the clerk's hearing his or her rights of appeal from the small claims judgment are severely limited by the lack of a more expansive appellate procedure available in the normal district court trial mechanism. Further, under this small claims system, the adverse judgment of the clerk, who may have made a number of legal errors in arriving at a decision, is introduced in the appeal trial, and thus it may lawfully taint the landlord's appeal from the very start of the case. In fact, the winning tenant need not introduce any evidence other than the decision of the clerk and may win on that evidence alone. Additionally, an appeal from a loss of the appeal is, in this author's opinion, next to impossible, because the judge hearing the landlord's appeal has virtually unfettered discretion to deny the landlord's motions for further appellate review of a loss.

Make no mistake, an appeal from an adverse small claims judgment is complex enough to warrant the retention of a lawyer, an expense the landlord sought to avoid in the first place. Since failure to pay a small claims judgment can carry a contempt penalty with the consequent loss of liberty, no landlord should blithely assent to remaining in the "velvet trap" of the small claims session simply because it is misnamed, "small claims." Treble damages could easily amount to $4500 or more (assuming rent to be $1500 per month), plus attorney's fees of the tenant (usually not less than $1200-$1500). Thus, such a judgment could easily total $6000. This author was recently hired to seek relief from the judgment after it had been appealed to a judge in the small *claims session, which, by that time, had grown to $12,000. There is nothing "small" about exposure to such monetary penalties and the threat of incarceration. Although the services of a lawyer may be necessary in opting out of the small claims session, this author urges landlords to do so pro se, or to at least hire an attorney to guide them through the relatively simple process of moving the court to transfer the case to the regular civil docket of the district court. See MASS. GEN. LAWS ch. 218, § 21-25.*

§ 9(h). Landlord's Appeal Bond from Small Claims Court.

The burdens of an appellant landlord in a security deposit appeal are intended to be onerous and obviously applied so as to discourage all but the most legitimate appeals. Such a defendant landlord must post a bond equal to three times the amount of the security deposit or three times the balance to which the tenant was entitled, plus interest at the rate of 5% from the date payment was due, with court costs and an amount to cover attorney's fees already expended or which may be expended during the course of the appeal. Despite it's draconian reach, this statutory scheme has been upheld as constitutional.[53]

---

[53] MASS. GEN. LAWS ch. 218, § 23; *Hampshire Village Associates v. District Court of Hampshire*, 381 Mass. 148, 153, 480 N.E.2d 830, 833 (1980) *cert. denied* 449 U.S. 1062 (1980): "If the § 15B provision for treble damages is taken to be free of constitutional doubt, then it follows with high probability that the provision of G. L. c. 218, § 23, for an appeal bond in roughly similar amount to protect that recovery is likewise constitutional."

§ 10. Landlord's Counterclaim for Damages.

In the ordinary course, where damage exists, the landlord would have a counterclaim for damage to the apartment, in a tenant's suit for security deposit violations, where the amount claimed exceeds the security deposit. However, if the landlord violates § 15B(6) by transgressing against any one of the following five rights of the tenant, he or she also forfeits the right to retain any portion of the security deposit for any reason and he or she also forfeits the right to counterclaim for any damage to the premises in any action brought by the tenant to recover the security deposit.

However, the appellate courts have made it clear that this poses no bar to the landlord's commencing an independent suit for tenant damage to the apartment.[54] The offenses are: (a) failure to properly deposit as per subsection (3); (b) failure to furnish within thirty days of the tenant vacating the premises the itemized list of damages and the other required documents; (c) failure to transfer the security deposit to the successor(s) in interest pursuant to § 15B(5); (d) failure to return the balance due in a timely fashion; or (e) use in any lease signed by the tenant of any provision which conflicts with § 15B and attempts to enforce such illegal provisions or to obtain waivers from a tenant of these protections.[55]

Additionally, the landlord incurs treble damages, interest at the rate of 5% from the date payment is due, and attorney's fees and costs for failing to properly escrow the deposit, for failing to properly transfer the security deposit to a successor owner, and for failing to properly return the

---

[54] Jinwala v. Bizzaro, 24 Mass. App. Ct. 1, 6-7, 505 N.E.2d 904, 907 (1987).

[55] MASS. GEN. LAWS ch. 186, § 15B(6).

deposit within 30 days of the termination of the tenancy as explained above and as required by subsection 6 of the statute.[56]

§ 11. Landlord's Right to a Key; Access.

At common law, where there is no agreement to the contrary, a landlord does not have the right to enter the premises without the tenant's permission.[57] Conversely, where there is agreement, a landlord may enter on agreed terms. The landlord may not enter the premises before termination of the tenancy under modern law except for these limited purposes: to inspect, to make repairs, and to show to prospective tenants, purchasers or mortgagees or their agents.[58] The landlord may inspect within the last thirty days of the tenancy "or after either party has given notice to the other of intention to terminate the tenancy," for the purpose of determining the amount of damage, only if the landlord is holding a security deposit.[59] The landlord may also enter "in accordance with a court order" or "if the premises appear to have been abandoned by the lessee." At common law it does not appear that the landlord has the right to have a key to the tenant's apartment absent an agreement to that effect. However, the standard Rental Housing Association lease and written tenancy at will agreement provide for the landlord's right to have a key and access on limited terms.

---

[56] MASS. GEN. LAWS ch. 186, § 15B(6),(7).

[57] Strycharski v. Spillane, 320 Mass. 382, 385, 69 N.E.2d 589, 591 (1946); Young v. Garwacki, 380 Mass. 162, 170, 402 N.E.2d 1045, 1050 (1980).

[58] MASS. GEN. LAWS ch. 186, § 15B(1)(a).

[59] *Id.*

§ 12. Penalty for Late Rent Payments.

Despite the fact that tenants often pay so late in the month that the landlord incurs late charges under the mortgage note, Chapter 186 bars the imposition in any rental agreement of interest or penalty "for failure to pay rent until thirty days after such rent shall have been due."[60]

§ 12(a). Remedy.

Although no forfeiture or monetary penalty exists in the statute to remedy a landlord's noncompliance, it is clear that failure to observe this subsection of the statute violates Chapter 93A and could therefore open the door to injunctive relief, reformation of the lease, money damages, costs and attorney's fees.[61]

§ 13. The Last Month's Rent.

A landlord who takes the last month's rent in advance is not burdened by as many record-keeping or escrow constraints as is a landlord who takes a security deposit. In light of this, many have chosen to forego the security deposit and simply take a last month's rent under the following terms and conditions.

---

[60] MASS. GEN. LAWS ch. 186, § 15B (1)(c).

[61] Mass. Regs. Code tit. 940, § 3.16(3). Section 93A is violated if an act or practice "fails to comply with existing statutes,... [is] meant for the protection of the public's health, safety, or welfare,... [is] intended to provide the consumers of this Commonwealth protection," or if "the act of practice otherwise fails to comply with the provisions of M.G.L. ch. 186, § 15B." *See id.*; MASS. GEN. LAWS. ch. 93A, §§ 2 and 9.

§ 13(a). Receipt.

Any landlord or agent taking "rent in advance for the last month of the tenancy" must give a receipt at the time of taking the last month's rent indicating the following: (1) the amount tendered; (2) date of receipt; (3) clear identification of the money as last month's rent; (4) name of the person receiving it; (5) the landlord for whom the money is received if taken by an agent; (6) a description of the premises for which the last month's rent is taken; (7) a statement indicating the tenant's entitlement to yearly interest at the rate of 5%; and (8) a statement telling the tenant he or she should provide a forwarding address by the end of the tenancy to which the interest may be sent.[62]

§ 13(b). Required Interest.

Interest must be paid over to the tenant either on the anniversary date of the tenancy at the rate of 5% (or such lesser percent as the landlord actually collects), or on a pro-rata basis for all months except the last month of the tenancy in the event the tenancy is terminated "before the anniversary date of such tenancy."

"At the end of each year of tenancy, such lessor shall give or send...a statement ... [indicating] the amount payable by such lessor to the tenant." The lessor is required to "give or send to such tenant the interest ... or shall notify the tenant that he may deduct the interest from the next rental payment." If the tenant has not received either the interest or the notice "after thirty days from the end of each year of the

---

[62] MASS. GEN. LAWS ch. 186, § 15B(2)(a).

tenancy," he or she may deduct the interest due from the next rental payment.[63]

§ 13(c). Remedy Upon Failure to Pay Interest on Last Month's Rent Within Thirty Days of Termination of Tenancy.

If once the tenancy is ended the landlord fails to pay interest due within thirty days after "termination of the tenancy," which logically means within thirty days of the tenant vacating the premises, in a suit against the landlord the tenant "shall be awarded damages in an amount equal to three times the amount of interest to which the tenant is entitled, together with court costs and reasonable attorney's fees."[64]

§ 13(d). Transfer of Last Month's Rent to Successor in Interest.

The lessor who holds a last month's rent, upon transfer of his interest in the property for any reason "whether by sale, assignment, death, appointment of a receiver or trustee in bankruptcy, or otherwise," must credit to his successor in interest, for the account of the tenant, the amount of the last month's rent, plus interest. [65] However, the grant of a mortgage on the subject premises by the lessor to a lender "shall not be deemed such a transfer of interest" as would trigger transfer duties. The successor in interest shall then credit the tenant with the last month's rent amount, plus interest, and he or she shall be liable for said last month's

---

[63] *Id.*

[64] *Id.*

[65] MASS. GEN. LAWS ch. 186, § 15B(7A).

rent, plus accrued interest, from the date of the property transfer unless and until either of the following events takes place.[66] See sections 13(e)-(h) below.

§ 13(e). Continuing Liability of the Lessor or His/Her Agent.

Despite transfer to the successor in interest, the lessor or his agent, presumably the property manager, continue to be liable for the last month's rent until one of the following occurs: (a) the last month's rent has been credited to the account of the tenant AND the tenant has been notified in writing of the "successor in interest's name, business address and business telephone number"; or (b) the successor in interest gives written notice in compliance with the requirements of the prior clause; or (c) the last month's rent has been credited to the tenant and all accrued interest has been paid to the tenant.[67]

§ 13(f). Successor in Interest's Duty to Notify Tenant of Receipt of Last Month's Rent.

Within forty-five days of transfer of the last month's rent, the successor in interest shall notify the tenant in writing that the last month's rent was credited to the tenant, and that the successor in interest has assumed responsibility for the last month's rent. The notice "shall" contain the "the lessor's name, business address and business telephone number, and the name, business address, and business telephone number of his agent, if any."[68]

---

[66] *Id.*
[67] *Id.*
[68] *Id.*

31

§ 13(g). Successor in Interest's Liability Where the Lessor Fails to Properly Credit the Last Month's Rent to the Successor in Interest.

If the lessor fails to properly credit the last month's rent to the tenant as provided in §15B(7A), without regard to the nature of the transfer giving rise to the successor in interest's duty to account under the statute, the successor in interest shall be liable to the tenant for the last month's rent, and he or she shall give the tenant credit for said last month's rent, plus accrued interest. As an alternative, if the tenant still resides in the premises in question, the successor in interest may discharge his or her obligations under the statute by allowing the tenant to reside without payment of rent for the period of time paid for by the last month's rent.[69]

§ 13(h). Exemptions from Last Month's Rent Obligations: Tenancies of 100 Days or Less for Vacation Rentals, Commercial Tenancies, Municipal Property Tax Foreclosures, Bank Foreclosures.

MASS. GEN. LAWS ch. 186, § 15B applies only to residential tenancies.[70] Further, the statute does not apply to

---

[69] *Id.*

[70] Shwachman v. Khoroshansky, 15 Mass. App. Ct. 1002, 448 N.E.2d 409 (1983). Where in spite of having executed a lease of commercial premises for commercial purposes, the lessee nonetheless used part of the commercial premises for living space, in contravention of the dictates of the lease and against the understanding of the lessor, the Appeals Court held that the lessee could not avail itself of the protections of MASS. GEN. LAWS ch. 186, § 15B due to the fact that despite the mixed nature of the use,

tenancies of 100 days or less of rentals for vacation or recreational purposes.[71] Lastly, a city or town which acquires the property through foreclosure of tax title or a "foreclosing mortgagee or a mortgagee in possession which is a financial institution chartered by the commonwealth or the United States" is exempt from successor in interest liability if the former owner fails to transfer the last month's rent in a proper and timely fashion. Therefore, none of the obligations described above regarding last month's rent apply in these situations.[72]

§ 14. Security Deposit - Bankruptcy Effect.

In a tenant's bankruptcy filing where "a lease provision establishing or security deposit to secure a lessee's obligation under a lease creates a debt of the landlord to the tenant contingent on the tenant's performance," the landlord may set off the amount of the security deposit against the tenant's pre-petition rental arrearage.[73] The landlord under these circumstances may take and retain the security deposit. The right to do so is granted under the Bankruptcy Code, not Massachusetts law.[74] The Code allows mutual pre-filing debts to be offset against one another unaffected by the

---

the statute was only intended and did indeed apply only to residential not commercial tenancies.

[71] MASS. GEN. LAWS ch. 186, § 15B(9): "The provisions of this section shall not apply to any lease, rental, occupancy or tenancy of one hundred days or less in duration which lease or rental is for a vacation or recreational purpose."

[72] MASS. GEN. LAWS ch. 186, § 15B(7A).

[73] In re Scionti, Inc., 40 B.R. 947 (D. Mass. 1984).

[74] 11 U.S.C. § 553 (2005).

Bankruptcy Code's bar against preferential treatment of certain transfers of the debtor's assets.[75]

The *Scionti* lease provision controlling the security deposit created a debt running from the landlord to the debtor-tenant.[76] So long as the tenant performed fully the security deposit remained the property of the tenant, and therefore a debt of the landlord to the tenant. However, where the bankrupt tenant fell behind in its obligations prior to filing, it created a pre-petition debt running in the landlord's favor. In that the Bankruptcy Code allows these pre-petition debts to be mutually offset, the landlord has the right to retain the security deposit to the full extent of the rental arrearage, without having the transfer set aside as "preferential" where the security deposit was applied within ninety days of the debtor-tenant's filing for bankruptcy.[77]

---

[75] 11 U.S.C. §§ 547, 553; In re Scionti, Inc., 40 B.R. 947, 948 (D. Mass. 1984).

[76] 40 B.R. 947, 948 (D. Mass. 1984).

[77] In re Scionti, Inc., 40 B.R. at 948 (D. Mass. 1984).